The Mermaids Visit the Vet

Written by Celia Warren
Illustrated by Jessica Secheret

Bella looked at
her pet fish, Twink.
Twink was sad.

“Let’s play with Twink,” said Anna.
“She will soon feel better.”

Anna's starfish went to play with Twink.
So did Henry, the crab.

But Twink did not want to play.

“Oh no!” said Bella.
“I think Twink is sick!”

“Let’s take her to the vet,” said Jo.

The mermaids went to see
Octopus, the vet.
Bella held Twink in her hands.

WELCOME
VET

They got to the vet's cave.
"Come in!" said Octopus.

Octopus looked at Twink's fins and tail.

They looked good.

"Twink has a sore tummy,"
said the vet.
"Poor Twink!" said Bella.

Then Octopus held Twink upside down!
"What are you doing?" said Bella.

Twink gave a hiccup.
Out came a little shell!
“Oh Twink!” said Bella.
“**That** is why you felt sick!”

“Thank you very much, Octopus!” said Bella.

Bella gave Twink a big hug.
"No more shells for you!" she said.